Where Flowers May Grow

Brittanie Watts

Published by Brittanie Watts, 2024.

WHERE FLOWERS MAY GROW

First edition. September 9, 2024.

ISBN: 979-8227404497

Written by Brittanie Watts.

I want to humbly thank my friends and family for their continued support and for putting up with hearing my new poems all the time. To my best friend since Pre-K Shelby without whom I wouldn't have this magnificent cover art to accentuate my works! Love you all!

I wasn't prepared for the devastation of a small tornado
You whipped through the wall I built to protect myself
You made me crumble
I scavenged the ground for my pieces
but they had blown away in the winds of your destruction
With a flicker, my light was dashed and my hope murdered
And while none of it bothered you
I felt the pain for both of us

I do not exist to boost the fragile egos of the male species

I was not born to walk on egg shells to prevent the shatter of your delicate mind

I will never water myself down

I am as sharp as the whiskey in your throat

It will burn as you swallow my words but know that it is only for the truth I speak

I am as raw as the honey that drips from bee hives though not as sweet

As unforgettable as the noose you found in your grandfathers attic at the age of 6

You didn't understand what you saw until years later

and you won't understand what you've lost until after I've left

because your talent is keeping your eyes closed until you've let go

Like seeds you planted the worms of distrust in my soul
Forged in the fires of your missteps
from those who have trespassed you
Yet I'm made to suffer from your suffering
When does it end?
When will the hurricane of your absence take to calm waters?
When does your tyranny die out
and the ones you've left in your wake stop suffering?

I have nightmares that rattle my bones
A cold chill cutting through my skin like butter
My teeth shatter like glass on the concrete of my difficult thoughts

I was a match that you ignited
you stepped away and watched me burn up
As the flames consumed me
so did the loneliness as I had lost your touch
Your arms were the only thing that could've contained the flames
but they had abandoned me
Wrapped around someone else

I've bled oceans for a man who wouldn't bleed a drop for me
I've broken my bones bending over backwards
I've cut my lips on the silence that I've tried to kiss off of his skin
I've crawled across hot embers on my bare knees
searching for the pieces of my heart that was demolished
in the roaring flames of his absence
I've shattered my teeth with the power of the words
that left from between them
and I was still silenced

One day you'll search for me
I won't be there for you to bury your sorrows in
I hate that I love you
You're the weak spot that I can't help but fall through

Nothing is more precious than the hours I spend wishing I had you
and nothing is more painful than the days that you give me your
silence in return
Searching for your hand in the dark
blindly reaching out but I do not find you
Where have you gone?
In the days that I count the stars
I count all of the things I love about you
How your smile lights up my world like a lighthouse at sea
How your laughter brings me joy and makes me feel like a thousand
butterflies are ready to burst out of my chest
And that look, those eyes, oh how they make me tremble inside
as if the world were coming to an end and you were my salvation
Your voice, your words, they drip like honey into my ears
so soft and sweet that I almost forget that the world is harsh
I dream of melting into you, of becoming yours forever
but you won't have me and it's killing me inside
When I say I miss you, you won't believe me
When I say I love you, you won't hear me
My cries for you fall upon deaf ears
I find myself shouting at a wall
with the hope that some day it'll crumble down

The poison of your words seeped into my skin
Buried itself into my very pores
no matter how hard I scrubbed
It never came off

I don't want to love you if that means feeling pain
I don't want to miss you if that means saying goodbye
I don't want to wake up one morning with you gone from my life
Falling for you even when I knew that your heart would never be
mine
How can I explain to you that I'd give you all of my time
If only the stars could count how much you mean to me
If the moon could shine light for you to see
That I would never walk away from you
if you let me be by your side
With every wave of the ocean I see you in the tide
If I could just get to you reach you just in time
but you're walking the other way and I'm not running fast enough
in your arms is where I want to be until the end of time

With a smile you opened up my wounded heart
I never knew it was so easy to open up and want someone
too used to being used to know anything other than numbness
but you gave me hope if only for a flicker of time
and like that, that small little flame burned out
carried away by the wind of the times changing
how could I have lost something so quickly I ask myself
losing hope and doubting myself every step
I felt the change before I outright noticed it
I thought I was going crazy
my friends told me I was overthinking it and then you faded away
without warning and I wasn't prepared for the devastation
They say to never let the pain make you harder
but if I don't become harder I'm going to crumble
until there's nothing left of me
I'm just supposed to pretend like It doesn't hurt
while none of it ever bothered you

This may be the last thing that I see
so I'll hold it fondly in my heart
This may be the last time that I breathe
so I'll breathe it all in
Pain and happiness and everything that surrounds me
I'll dance in these rain clouds that seem to hover over me wherever I
go
If I should fall asleep tonight and not wake up tomorrow
just remember me for all the laughs we had and all the tears we
shared

You picked at me like a scab
Used me like spare parts
You said I was the damaged one
but you were the one who ripped me up
and tossed me aside
You use the word crazy like a bandage
to cover up the wounds you lashed into my chest

Sweet lies thick like honey
drip from the mouths of men
who pry our legs open to feel something other than their own despair
Their hungry hands grip our bodies like the trophies they won't ever
obtain
Tearing at our bodies trying to take pieces into the empty spaces in
their minds
And we let them
we spread our legs and let them fill the void that the men before left
in our hearts
We tell ourselves that everything will be okay
but that lie falls away
like ashes from cigarettes that are lifted to mourning lips

If I die before I meet your lips
I'll be burning in my grave
You've made it clear
That it's not me that you crave
Though I long for your touch
I've let you go away
I have to set you free
I know you don't wish to stay
You were just the bird
That my heart wanted to cage

You're the reason I cry myself to sleep at night
The reason I wake up and I can't breathe
You haunt every empty space in my heart and trespass in every corner
of my soul
I can't take a step without being reminded of you
When did breathing become so painful?
When did I start regretting every beat of my heart?
The moment your silence became deafening, I became absent
I became empty like an abandoned house
I searched for an occupant but no one wanted to stay
They filled the void you left for a little while and then disappeared
Like the smoke from the cigarettes I smoke to destroy myself
You taught me to destroy myself

We look to ourselves so empty and bare
and no one gives a shit
so why should we care
and we look to the sky
and scream
THIS ISN'T FAIR
as if someone could ever hear us up there

I'm drowning in the pain inflicted by thoughts of you
my body is my prison and I can't escape
this flesh covered cage entraps me
I take foreign bodies who pass through my life
like shadows just to feel something
anything
but they never reach my core
that ball of ice that makes me shiver in my sleep
I'm so numb and lost

Maybe you'll notice that I don't laugh anymore
That my smile no longer meets my eyes
or maybe you won't at all
Maybe the sadness will overflow my sight
And you won't see me disappear into myself
As the sorrow seeps from my eyes
It gives my cheek a final embrace
And I wonder if I could ever break free
From these chains that bind me

The time was ready but my heart was not
And every time I think of you, my breath it stops
Like a parasite you invade my every thought
The time it drags on, tick tock tick tock
You swim in my head as if it were made for you
I beg you to leave but you don't want to
And every time I walk away and say that I'm through
There's always something that drags me back to you
It's like a tragedy repeating in my head
Thinking of every moment and where it's lead
Hanging on to every word you've ever said
It's days like this that I wish I was dead
My heart it drains with every tear I cry
Trying so damn hard to say goodbye
But no matter what I do or how hard I try
Your memory, the pain, it just won't die
Now I'm left here with your knife stuck in my heart
You painted me with blood and called it art
I was your science experiment, you took me apart
You were my end and I was your start

Don't cry at my funeral
Your tears won't water my grave
Your memories cannot bring me back
I wasn't yours to save
Surrounded by people
Yet I felt so alone
The dark lonely place in my head
Was the place I called home
Friends with the demons
Who danced inside my head
They wanted nothing more for me
Than for me to be dead
And I'll admit
Maybe it wasn't my time
But those tidal waves of pain
Washed me over the shoreline
I'd find myself thinking
That I'd be better off dead
It was easier than fighting
With the war inside my head
Tired eyes and sad smiles
How did you not notice the war behind my eyes

You were wrapped
In caution tape
The day I met you
I thought that if I peeled it back
I'd find someone worth saving
Instead I found myself
Wrapped in fragile tape
The moment you broke free

I felt my sanity slip
It was slight at first
Then all at once
I grasped for straws
To keep it around
I felt the shift
Like an earthquake
The ground broke
From beneath my feet
I don't recognize myself anymore

I've been breaking vows
I swore always to keep
I'm wide awake even when my eyes
Feel like they're going to explode
I do not recognize the person
I lie in bed with
I wake up
I look in the mirror
I recognize the face
The body along with it
But I'm trapped in this mind
With someone else
They feel lighter
But they are darker
I am afraid

I sit in this house
We built together
Everything seems dingy
Without you here
Our memories
Painted on the walls
I'm crumpled up
Like a piece of paper
Someone discarded

I am a haunted house
Full of ghosts from my past
Men knock on my door
But they don't dare enter
For fear that they too
Will become one of the ghosts
Trapped

Chasing you
is like running
Into a brick wall
Repeatedly
Expecting it to
Crumble

You didn't think
That your silence
Made a sound
But I heard it
All too clear
I understood
What it meant

Why am I satisfied
With receiving crumbs
When there's someone out there
Who will give me a whole sandwich

A house of sadness
Built just for me
It's walls of paper
Cut my skin
My blood paints it's floors
And still it's my home

I gave so much
Of my kindness away
I forgot to spare
Some for myself

Your anger
Scorched my skin
With such an intensity
That it left scars

Ashes to ashes
I fall down
At the feet of the fire
Where you burned my hope

The way you look at me
Tells me that you want me
But you're trying to convince me
That I do not stand a chance
In my mind you have started a war
The left side of my brain
Is saying to wait
The right side is saying
I should move on
My heart screams
In protest
My body has become a war zone

The first time your hands
Left marks on my skin
The first time you cried and promised
You'd never do it again
You made me believe
That's what love was

Swallowed by pain
Alone in the dark
In fear I breathe solemnly
For what is to come
Will surely come to stay
It will blot out the sky
The sun will shine no longer
Darkness will consume me
Alone in the dark
Swallowed by pain

Were you there
To see me shatter?
You walked away
Did I even matter?
Promised me your heart
You let me wither and die
My chest is hollow
From all the tears I cried
Like a wilting flower
I grew darker and dark
I am cold and lifeless
No such thing as a spark
My mind is set on vengeance
I became cold inside
I used to be so full of love
But you're the reason it died
I will wilt every spark
Of happiness you find
I will make you feel
What I do inside

I still do not know what safety is
I keep finding myself wrapped in arms
That crush my ribs

The rain kisses the ground
I'm reminded of your lips
And how they'll never meet mine again
How your body
Will never know the love that mine can give
Or how your heart will never know
The passion so pure that it scorches my veins
My heart threatens to burst
when I see you

I tasted the withdrawal on your lips
As I wasted the last night with you
Wishing I had not been so naive
You didn't see the flowers
I was willing to grow for you
Didn't bother to tell me
Just one word of honesty
I was not worth the truth to you
I was not worth one moment
Of the silence you would not break
You spun bullshit excuses
While I believed in your bullshit lies
What a mess that's been created

I tried to show you
The art that my body housed
But you had sewn your eyes shut
I tried to sing you
The beautiful melodies of my heart
But you covered your ears
I tried to kiss
The silence off your lips
But you glued them together

July 22nd
The day that the future I had painted for us
Started to melt into reality
As your lies found truth and my eyes opened
Taking a small portion of the person
I had built myself up to be

It's funny how the first
Show you asked me to watch
Related to the skeletons you kept in your closet
How you deceitfully played along
You pretended you were just like me
Now the skeletons are roaming the halls
Of your abandoned mind
I wonder if you realize
That soon everyone will see them

This depression and anxiety
Living rent free inside my body
I try to run to just be free
I'm running out of space, suffocating
"How could someone ever love you?"
"You aren't worth anything to anyone"
"Why don't you just die, no one will miss you"
Those are the things they tell me when I'm alone
I choke back the tears I'm drowning in
Hold in the cries for help that claw at my throat
I believe these things they tell me
There's no fixing me, I'm broken

Sometimes I want to drown
In the pool of sadness that I seem to be floating in
I dream of sinking to the bottom
Hoping that someday, it will all end
That I will end
Emotions slice into my chest, marking
Like the words that scar my body
They say to keep my head up
But what will I say when my neck has grown tired?
What will I do when I become tired of being trapped?
I wonder when will my knees buckle
under all the pressure
It's like an inevitable tidal wave
coming to knock me down and drag me under
They say I have a choice to be in this spot
I say to them
speak to the depression who has my feet glued

Her origami shape
Elegantly waltzes
Into the dreams of men
Sways them
Falling for her is poisonous
Because though she is a dream by night
By day she crumbles
For she is truly no shape at all
She rises and she falls
She grows and she shrinks

You hide monsters in your closet
Like I hide secrets in my heart
You grabbed my hand and smiled
Before you ripped my world apart
Letting go of what I thought could be
I'm left here with my own grief
And it's all my own damn fault
You had no hesitations to leave
Picking you off my mind piece by piece
While also trying to hold onto my heart
I'll rise above this one day
And I'll thank you for tearing me apart

I'm an over thinker
I tear things apart to understand
I pick at scabs to see all parts of the wound

It's in these moments that I realize
how truly alone I really am
How the thoughts gnaw at me
until I'm raw and wet from the tears
that have soaked my hair and the pillow under me
How easy is it to say goodbye
but how hard it is to walk away
That feeling of my heart sinking so low
that I fear it will set like the sun
and it won't ever rise again
Oh how I wish I would never rise again
For every breath I take, the deeper my pain runs
Time does not heal, it only brings more longing

You claimed me like a trophy you were never meant to win
When the glory died down
you threw me out like wasted dreams

So thin
Sunken in
Like a skeleton
With paper for skin
I watch you disappear

I've contemplated my reasons for staying
I've made lists in my head
But each number is like a staple in my heart
Reminding me why I'm trapped
A list of reasons why I'm doomed to suffer a lifetime

I just don't feel the same
And I think that bothers people
They look at me with judgment screaming in their eyes
Beg me to heed their words like they're a testament
I feel so small and inferior
Why do I feel as though I'm not allowed to grow
from the concrete that's tried to define me
I look to them as they cast down on me
I wither again

I'm calling your name from the depths of my soul
and yet you turn and say it's better if you go
I didn't think that this would hurt so fucking bad
Are you missing me and all that we had?
When my time comes and I'm finally at rest
Will I finally have your caress?
Will you look upon my face and kiss my cheek
Knowing that in my darkest times, you chose to leave

Your head is laid on my chest and I wonder if you can hear my heart screaming out for help

Did you not taste the salt on my cheeks

Like an ocean this pain sloshes around in my chest and I wonder if you can hear the tidal waves crashing into my soul

It's like I'm invisible
Standing on the shoreline
I'm going to dive in and no one will see me
I'll disappear under the current
and get lost in the frigid waves of forgotten
that's where I'll stay
Where I'll chose to be buried
and where I'll beg to remain

You dashed my dreams and put out this fire behind my eyes
And I allowed you to come into my house of peace and destroy me
I watched as you tore my art from the walls
I stood unblinking as you shattered my vases of roses
I only really cried when you walked back out the door
and left me with my torment

I am a rose with thorns
I was not made to love easy
I was made so that the ones
who were willing to work for my love
were to be the ones who deserved
the immense out flowing of love channeled
through each of my delicate petals
men were not made to pluck

Like cancer you latched onto my heart and devoured my life
Your memory, a parasite worming through my head
Your ghost still haunts the halls of the empty house I live in
You make me sick to my stomach
I'm trying so hard to vomit back up these feelings I have for you

I could travel the 7 seas
explore the whole world in search for your love but I will never find
it

Your lies suffocate me
Your false claim on your love for me, chokes me
But I know that in your eyes
I will never be worth anymore than what my body can offer to you.
I was a chess piece in your game of bullshit.
How you love to watch me bleed for you
Your smile growing wider with every inch of pain I gift you
The rivers I've bled for you will never quench your thirst
The tears I've cried for you will never be sufficient
And yet, I keep mourning you
How dreadful a one sided love can be

It's not your words that terrify me but how easy they are to swallow
and I begin to wonder if there will ever be an edge of truth in any of

it

I wish with every bone of my body that you choke on every lie
that tries to thrust itself from between your lips
All I've ever known are men with empty promises
and hollow eyes that promise the world
but take until I've nothing more to give
Forgive me if I cannot trust any song
you try to sing into my cold dead chest

I look at your picture
All I see is my regret
To forget you is something
I haven't figured out yet
I'm mourning you
And you aren't even dead
What's it going to take
To get you out of my head
I find myself at the bottom of the bottle
And I still can't look up
I'm drowning away my sorrows
Thinking about this breakup
I want to scream and say I'm done
But I keep coming back for more
How many times do I have to break
Before I learn to close the door
You keep knocking saying to open up
And I just let you in
"I'm so fucking sick of this shit"
I say while sipping on gin
I'm feeling warm inside
But cold in my heart
I bet it's just a show for you
Come watch me fall apart.

You ripped up my emotions
Like a piece of paper
You didn't take a second glance
Before you tossed them aside
And walked away

In free fall
Down a dark tunnel
Cold and alone
I'm unafraid
And that's what scares me the most
I'm spiraling
Spinning out of control
I'm sinking fast
Into a pit of depression
Melting into myself
I become disfigured
I've lost myself again

When I hold you
You're like ashes crumbling in my hands
Slipping through and blowing away
I wonder if I'm gripping you too tight
If my passion is burning too hot
I feel as though I'm too much
As if I can't hold anything without destroying it

When you tell me goodbye
Let it not be with razor sharp teeth
Dicing up words and spitting them out
As if they mean nothing to you
Take care with the poison
You carelessly spew
When you tell me goodbye
Try not to choke on the silence
That will stalk you in my wake

I don't recognize myself anymore
Can't handle what I'm seeing
Falling to the floor
Looking for an exit
I can't reach the door
I'm screaming out for help
I'm trapped inside
No one listens anymore
I'm swept away with the tide
Rolling angry waves
Sloshing and crashing
My spark fades
Drifting further away
Cold and alone
I don't want to stay

Depression built the room
I lay my head in
Full of thoughts of failure
You'll see my motivation got lost
In the mountain of clothes
Some unfolded and some unwashed
The trash on the floor
Is just a depiction
Of how I see myself
Unimportant and worthless

I was only 13
But I remember
How small you made me feel
Sweaty palm
Clamped down hard
Covering my mouth
As I tried to scream
I remember
The pain you made me feel
As you invaded my body
The fight I had
Was not enough
You took my dignity
You stole my innocence

When you said forever
You meant with me
Except you didn't anticipate
That I was only half a person
How could I blame you
Half a person
Couldn't have been good enough
Not even for myself

I'm stretched paper thin
I feel my mother
collecting pieces of me
trying to glue me back together
Trying to keep me from sinking
to the bottom of my sorrow
I feel as though she can feel me slipping away I'm disintegrating in
my pain
she glimpsed my soul through the windows
I didn't mean to open
My tears gushing out
and I believe that it was then
that she seen my truth

I've never fully trusted
A living soul
I've picked pieces off
But never the whole truth
I've judged what I could trust
And gathered what I could provide
I've never given someone the entirety
How can I trust anyone
With the shattered remains
Of the people who have betrayed me
They will surely betray me as well
Sometimes the weight of my own truth
Finds me and crushes me
Until I'm a puddle of tears

I nurture and feed
Your absence
As if it's mouth is open
Hungry for my attention
I try to gather myself
And walk away from the seat
You used to occupy
But in the dim light of my existence
I see your ghost
The flower of hope
That rests in my chest
Hasn't withered away yet
I water it with poison against you
Hoping for it's demise
So I can regain control
And be free of your hold

I reach for your shadow
As if it's flesh and bones
I try to hold onto it's sharp edges
Hoping to feel the smallest hint of you
But all I get are wounds
I beg myself to let go

I used to smile
about how your eyes changed colors
like the seasons
but what I didn't realize
was that your heart did too

I've contemplated suicide thought of all the ways
I could go out
paced wall to wall
Talked myself into it
Talked myself out of it
Monotonously counting
Reasons to stay
Counting reasons to go
Keeping score to justify

Depression has built its nest
Inside of my chest
Grown comfortable in my skin
Growing and squirming within
It has my body paralyzed
I'm glued in place
Mourning my dreams
As they pass me by
Looking for a savior
In every face I meet
I'm hopeless

You've left hollow voids
All of the places in my life you took up
Are now empty
I'm full of craters
I sometimes forget that you don't exist
In those moments, I relive losing you
I get that sinking feeling in my stomach
As my world falls over again
And reality spits in my face

I'll miss you in every breeze
That doesn't carry your voice
In every ray of sunshine
That doesn't bounce off your skin
In every melody that isn't sung from your lips
I'll think of you in all the places
I have come to know you
That's where I'll find you again

Your body left more than
Imprints in my bed
You laid in the empty spaces
That surround me
It feels so cold
So empty and bare
I reach for you in the dark
I'm grasping at air

How do you hide
Such a violent war
When chaos tries to coax
It out of the shadows
Tugging at every corner
Like a child tugs at her mothers skirt

Your words deceive me
My healing heart
Sought solace
In the idea of your company
You never planned
To give me your time
I was your entertainment
Until you got bored
Just a little pawn
In your game

You light a wildfire
Inside my chest
My body burns for you
We could set this town on fire
Set it ablaze and run away together

Are we just filling
The empty spaces
To pretend that we aren't lonely
The clocks been ticking loud
My ears are growing tired
I just want to rest my head a minute
In your lap of make believe

Good
But not good enough
Good enough to want
Never good enough to keep
Good enough to desire
Good enough to sleep with
Never good enough to love

I could rip out my vocal cords
I have no use for them
I could scream for hours
No one would come
There's no white knight
No one in shining armor to save you
These days you try to fly
And land flat on your face

I will paint you into every picture that I see
Even though you'll never see it
I will sing your name into every song I hear
Even though you'll never hear it
I will write your name in every book I read
Even though you will never read it
I will wove memories of you in everything I make
Even though you'll never touch them
Even though you never asked for it
I've accepted that you'll never be mine

In steady decline
Trying to define
What it means to live
When I have nothing to give
Death please come
In peaceful slumber

About the Author

I have struggled with severe depression and anxiety for many years. When I was only 8 years old, I started to write about my pain through poetry. I struggled with self harm and a few attempts at suicide which thankfully were not sucessful as I would not be here sharing with you my most intimate thoughts. I've lived through a lot and I've experienced a lot. I have not yet been able to write about some of the things I've experienced but I hope to gain the courage from my readers to do so.

www.ingramcontent.com/pod-product-compliance
Lightning Source LLC
Chambersburg PA
CBHW051758130726
47987CB00003B/1016